A COMPLETE GUIDE TO MANAGING AND CONTROLLING THE OUTCOME OF YOUR INSURANCE CLAIM

.

A COMPLETE GUIDE TO MANAGING AND CONTROLLING THE OUTCOME OF YOUR INSURANCE CLAIM

WILLIAM FISCHER

LIBRARY OF CONGRESS CONTROL NUMBER: 2011907733
ISBN: HARDCOVER   978-1-4628-7196-4
               SOFTCOVER   978-1-4628-7195-7
               EBOOK   978-1-4628-7197-1

To order additional copies of this book, contact:
Xlibris Corporation
1-888-795-4274
www.Xlibris.com
Orders@Xlibris.com
98515

CONTENTS

Homeowner's Quotes

- *I had a large fire in my home and was staying at a temporary location for one year. Mr. Fischer's book truly taught me how to manage all the information I received throughout the claim process and take the control out of the insurance company's hands and back into mine. All my friends now have a copy of his book. So if they ever have a claim, they will be better able to address all the issues they will be confronted with.*

Betty—Chicago, IL

- *I was displaced out of my home after a fire occurred for approximately 8 months. Although I consider myself a very organized individual, the amount of documentation I was receiving throughout the claim process was very overwhelming. After reading this book, I created the Homeowner's Claim Binder which is recommended for all homeowners to use and it allowed me to stay organized and address all the issues on a timely basis. Everyone should have one even prior to having an insurance claim.*

Khalila—Chicago, IL

- *I was so overwhelmed by contractors and public adjusters approaching me immediately after the fire to sign a contract. I used the techniques in this book to sort through all the solicitors and chose the right contractor to complete the repairs to my home. Thank you so much . . .*

Mary—Chicago, IL

- *I have had friends and family members over the years' experience the trauma of having a large fire at their home. It is without a doubt one of the single most tragic events that an individual can go through in their life. I tried the best I could, as a friend and relative, to be there for them and help them during the claim process. After reading this book, I was amazed how accurate the claim process was explained and how all the scenarios between the homeowner, contractor and insurance agent did indeed happen just how it was outlined in the book. I strongly recommend this book to all homeowners and encourage them to read it and be prepared! None of my family or friends ever thought they would have a fire. It only happens to other people! Well, they found out what really happens during the claim process the hard way. Don't you make the same mistake!*

Tony Carter, Chicago, IL

-President and Owner of "Take Note Construction";
-Twenty-one year veteran of the Insurance and Restoration Industry;
-Author of the motivational book "Determined to Rise"

I would like to dedicate this book to my daughter
and son, Sarah and Michael.

PREFACE

Let's think about what makes sense. If you are working on a personal budget to control your family's expenses, is it best to do it prior to or during a financial crisis? If you know you are having car problems, do you take it to an auto shop prior to a long trip or after your car has broken down during the trip? If your home, which represents one of the biggest investments of your life, is damaged by a sudden loss, do you want to learn what the insurance company is going to do to help you at *that* moment, or would you already like to know before it happens?

This book is written in terms that will be easily understood by the average homeowner. It does not include a lot of insurance policy jargon. Its purpose is to explain the insurance claim process in simple terms with many examples to illustrate the inner workings within the insurance company throughout the claim process.

This book will prepare a homeowner to address a wide variety of issues confronted from start to finish once a claim has been filed. It will also give you examples of forms you may be asked to fill out with easy-to-read instructions. It also gives you extensive lists of personal belongings that are in most homes, room by room, to help you fill out your inventory forms when the insurance company requests that you do so.

Take complete control throughout the claim process *out* of the insurance company's hands and *back* into yours. Be prepared and able to know not only the answers to many questions you will be asking during this process but know also what to expect from insurance companies, insurance agents, claim representatives, and contractors *before* it happens!

This is *your* time now. Manage and control the outcome of your insurance claim!

ABOUT THE BOOK

I want to make clear that the purpose of this book is not to attack or defend the insurance industry. Its purpose is to point out quite simply the claim process that most insurance companies follow and the impact it has on its policyholders. I will discuss how to manage your claim to ensure that the outcome is fair and that the maximum payment has been issued from the insurance company.

My background is heavily concentrated in the running of business operations and the delivery of a high level of service to customers. This includes over fifteen years in retail management; ten years in real estate including purchasing, reconstructing, and selling and renting of single-family homes; and last but not least, over ten years as a claim representative with one of the largest insurance companies in the United States of America.

This diverse background allowed me to have a well-rounded view throughout my claim representative career. It allowed me to understand not only the insurance side of the business but also the contractors who perform the reconstruction on the homes. It also allowed me to empathize with the policyholders who have to deal with both the pressures of dealing with the insurance company and contractors.

As most people know, when you are being trained by an individual during a company's training period, a lot of their philosophies and knowledge rubs off on you while training with them. You're like a sponge just waiting to soak in information. Good or bad, it becomes a foundation that you build on and affects what type of employee you will be later on.

I had a fellow claim representative state to me while training, "If you are thinking of denying a claim, picture yourself and the policyholder in front of a judge. The judge turns to you and asks if you are 100 percent sure that this loss is not covered. If you *cannot* honestly say you are 100 percent sure, pay the claim. The judge will side with the policyholder every time if you don't." This logic not only remained in my mind as a claim representative for the next decade but also taught me to address each claim with the thought that unless it is overwhelmingly evident that it is not covered, I am paying it.

I felt that my role as a claim representative was to represent the policyholder and give them every chance to provide documentation showing me that a loss had occurred.

This book is designed to educate the policyholder in every aspect of the claim process so there will be few surprises or curveballs thrown at them during this trying time.

A large house fire is one of the most tragic events that one can go through. Not only are you now homeless but you have also lost all the items precious to you that represent memories of years past. No insurance company can bring back family photos and videos, the first picture your child drew, or your pet that you saved from the animal shelter years ago. How can you get through this challenging time?

Be strong, be educated, and know your options and ensure that you *will* be made whole after this ordeal is over. Know that you are not alone, and there are resources out there to help you regain your life back. This book is one of them.

BRIEF HISTORY OF INSURANCE

The origins of insurance trace back to seventeenth-century England when merchants made arrangements to cover their potential losses of cargo during trade. Lloyds of London became the first insurance company in the Atlantic world. Lloyds was actually named after a coffee shop where the underwriters would meet to exchange news.

In America in the mid-1700s, houses were almost entirely made out of wood. Many of the settlements within the cities were built very close together. It started out to be for security reasons. Then as the cities grew, developers also built homes very close but for different reasons. They wanted to fit as many homes on their development lot as possible. Due to the materials they used to build these homes, the risk of a fire became more likely.

The Philadelphia Contributionship for the Insurance of Houses from Loss of Fire became the first mutual fire company in America. They set new standards for building houses by refusing to insure houses that were considered fire hazards.

Insurance is always in demand because people are always looking for ways to minimize risk. The Internet opened the door for people, giving them the ability to go online and find the cheapest rate. A business can even go online and check internationally for the right coverage.

There are several types of insurance available to protect consumers: health insurance, life insurance, auto insurance, and homeowner's insurance. These are just a few but probably the most well-known types to most individuals.

There are probably as many *large* insurance companies available as there are policies to choose from. Just because an insurance company is very large or strong does not mean it cannot be affected when a disaster strikes. A larger company can spread the cost of claims out, which allows them to offer coverage at lower prices. A smaller insurance company may be able to offer more personal service than the giants.

Most of the homeowner policies that are offered by these insurance companies are very similar. It is the level of service once a claim is filed that separates them from each other. All insurance companies have a claims department. But fewer have claim representatives that are available to respond to large losses. They need to hire an adjusting firm to represent them.

Although a claim can be handled properly through these firms, the individual adjuster who is assigned to meet you and write an estimate has very little control over the outcome of the claim. They are often used by your insurance company to gather information concerning your property loss.

The claim process usually will take longer because the adjusting firm needs to complete their investigation, generate an estimate, and forward this information to the claim representative in your insurance company for their review. Often these delays result in frustration for the policyholder and his or her hired contractor.

The best advice is to keep in touch with both the adjusting firm and your insurance company's claim representative and request frequent updates.

INSURANCE COMPANIES

FACT OR FICTION

There are countless books on the market today that discuss insurance companies and their practices. Most of them give multiple examples of abuse and distrust with the overall industry. Once again, I am not here to defend or attack the insurance companies. In fact, I could probably write a book with documented facts taking either approach, defending or attacking, and be just as persuasive in each.

I would like to point out in this section the most common phrases or statements the average homeowner states about insurance companies and the claim process and clarify the validity of them.

1. The insurance company is out to make money. That is their top priority.

FACT

The insurance company *is* a business like any other business. Their mere existence is based on making a profit. Without one, they will no longer be around. They have expenses and overhead just like any other business that must be managed in order to survive. They have a sales force—insurance agents, one-on-one service representatives—claim representatives, underwriters who review individual policies to ensure that the policies are profitable, supervisors that manage employees and oversee territories assigned to them, and much more.

The question is, how much money is ethical to make off your policyholders? How do they remain profitable? By controlling expenses and training their agents and claim representatives to pay what is owed? Or by paying less than owed or denying coverage on an insured loss? This is a debate that will probably go on forever.

2.   The insurance companies train their claim representatives to write low estimates for repairs and to deny claims as often as possible to keep expenses down and profits high.

FICTION

The insurance companies collect a premium every year that accumulates over time on behalf of the policyholder. This money is invested by insurance companies and used to generate income over the years. Many people believe that the insurance companies train their claim representatives to delay paying claims to allow these premiums maximum time to be invested by the company. Also, many say that claim representatives are trained to deny claims quickly so no payment will be made.

Over the decade that I was a claim representative, I took countless classes on claim handling. Training was a big priority so a claim representative could be as educated on the claim process as possible. At no time was there ever an instructor or supervisor who encouraged us to delay or deny a claim. Writing an accurate estimate was always a priority, and understanding the policy inside and out was mandatory so we could properly review a filed claim and come to a proper rendering at the conclusion.

Please note though that it is unlikely that two claim representatives, if assigned the same claim, would handle it identically. They may not even come to the same conclusion. How can this be if they were both trained in the same classrooms and seminars? I will discuss that in the chapter titled "The Claim Representative."

3.   If I file a claim, the insurance company may raise my premium or, even worse, cancel my policy.

FACT

There are so many factors that are considered when determining if a policy should remain enforced, to raise a premium or to cancel it. It is true that there are countless incidences where a policyholder has been a long-time customer who paid their premium every year and, after a large fire, are told that their policy is canceled.

The main reason for canceling a policy for a homeowner is that it is no longer profitable. For example, for over thirty years, a person pays $800 a year in premium. That is $24,000 in accumulated money on your behalf. Now you have a small loss in the amount of $4,000. You have paid into the insurance company over years *more* than they are paying out on this loss. Typically, you will not be canceled.

Same scenario as above, you have a large fire, and the payment from the insurance company is $100,000. The amount you have paid over the years is *less* than the amount being paid out. There is a strong probability your policy will be canceled.

If you have several small claims that are slowly adding up toward the total amount you have paid over the years, this tends to trigger your premium to be raised. This way, the insurance company can adjust your premium to compensate for the frequent claims.

There are so many other factors that play a role in determining the cancelation process and increase in premiums. The main thought process is, "Is this policy making or costing us money?" Is this wrong? How long can you run a business losing money? You decide.

4. The insurance adjusters are given bonuses based on how many denials they make.

FICTION

I hear this so frequently in the industry. It is absolutely false. There are so many "watchdog groups" overseeing the insurance industry. If any company rewarded their claim representatives based on the amount of denials they wrote, they would be shut down so fast that when the employees went to work the next day, the doors would already be chained and locked.

Every denial has to be explained and documented and reviewed by a supervisor. Once again, one claim representative may go to a loss and deny it and another may find coverage. This is a *major* problem in the industry that will be covered in succeeding chapters.

5. When a claim representative depreciates a building estimate or a list of damaged personal property, this process is not as objective as the insurance company states.

FACT

The topic of *depreciation* will be discussed in depth in future chapters, but subjectivity from the claim representative definitely plays a role. Although you will be told that depreciation is applied based on the age/life expectancy of the building material or personal property, this is a very gray area in the insurance industry.

Depreciation works like this. Let us say, for example, a typical flat-screen television tends to break down and is replaced after five years. So its average life span is five years. You have a fire and the television is damaged. It is two and a half years old. It has lived half of its expected life span. So if the brand-new television is worth $1,000, it is only worth $500 now—half its value because, presently, it's at half its life span. Simple.

This philosophy is the same for all personal contents and building materials throughout a home.

What is interesting is that after you receive your depreciated building estimate or personal property inventory, there is a very good chance you will find inconsistencies throughout. Many claim adjusters do not take in account the ages/life expectancies when calculating depreciation. New items just purchased or items under one year old will be depreciated where none should be. Even worse, many claim representatives depreciate the same amount or percent across the board because it's easier or faster. For example, they may apply 30 percent depreciation on all building materials damaged regardless of the age. This is absolutely wrong and is done frequently to policyholders throughout the industry. As I stated previously, I will discuss in more details this depreciation process in later chapters.

6.   The contractors that the insurance companies recommend are better qualified to do repairs than the ones you may find on the Internet or referred to you by friends.

FICTION

This is also a topic I devote an entire chapter on later in my book. These contractors have been reviewed closely by insurance companies and, for the most part, would not be recommended if they felt that they would receive complaints from policyholders about their work. Unfortunately, a program that supports a list of preferred contractors is designed to save money over time due to their purchasing power at specified retail outlets. When all the contractors buy building materials from these stores, the insurance company receives purchasing discounts. These discounts save millions of dollars over time and positively affect the bottom line of the company. Is this wrong? When a program is set in place with the main priority being financial gain/savings and customer service is second on the list, I think there can be a conflict of interest. As said earlier, we will discuss this in more length in a later chapter.

There are many contractors *not* listed as preferred contractors with the insurance company that do qualified work. They have greater flexibility in controlling the cost of their materials because they can buy materials anywhere. This cost savings can play a big part for a policyholder in negotiating with a contractor when it comes down to doing repairs to their home after the insurance check has been issued.

7.   A claim should be filed when a loss occurs at my home that is substantially over my deductible. If it is a small loss, it's best not to file a claim.

FACT

I cannot tell you how many times I have been approached over the years and asked, "I have a loss at my home. Should I file a claim?" Initially, there is no quick answer to this question. But with a little more information about the loss, it can be addressed.

Whether we like it or not, the frequency we file claims as a homeowner does raise an eyebrow with the insurance company. A homeowner needs to understand that claims were designed to be filed when a financial tragedy/loss occurs to your home. It was not designed for the maintenance and up keep of your home over the years. It would be a shame to have your policy canceled due to frequency of filing claims when a large fire could be just around the corner.

After your deductible has been applied, if the money that is given to you from the insurance company is not enough to pay for the damages, do *not* file a claim. It makes no sense. Forget about the fact that you have a policy and the insurance company should pay you for these repairs. This sort of thinking can cost you heavily if you are canceled. File a claim when the financial burden to repair is so great that you could never afford to do it yourself.

8.   Once the insurance company finishes with their investigation and writes their estimate for repairs, their decision on how much to pay is final.

FICTION

Most people look at their insurance company as this intimidating force that dictates exactly what your final settlement will be. That you have little to no control. This is incorrect. You have more control than you realize.

If you were in the landscaping business and a homeowner wanted a quote from you, you would have a better chance of getting the job, even if your price is higher, if you detail out all the work you plan on doing. Put prices next to each line item. Show the owner that not only do the trees have to come down but the stumps also have to be removed, and further work to the earth needs to be done. Maybe the other bids are lower, but they exclude some of the work that is essential to properly complete the job.

An estimate from a claim representative is just that. An estimate. It is unlikely that the claim representative has personally done the type of work they are estimating repairs for. They have had extensive training in identifying damages and taught how to apply traditional repairs to the damaged area. But they may be missing details that only a tradesman would know and must be included to properly do the work. Getting bids from contractors is essential to negotiate an insurance company's estimate.

Public adjusters are licensed companies who can legally represent you throughout the claim process. They know the policies very well and are either a licensed contractor or are affiliated with one. They can get bids from contractors who understand all of what entails on a particular job and help you get paid a proper amount for your loss.

Please note that like any business, a public adjuster does not volunteer to help based on the kindness of their heart. They, as well as the contractor, will be making a profit out of the check that is issued from the insurance company. Realize that you are now no longer getting the full settlement from the insurance company. A portion, directly or indirectly, is going to the public adjuster. Is this wrong? Not as long as all the work that was promised to be done to your home is indeed performed. Once again, you *must* understand the estimate written and follow up that all required work is being completed.

THE HOMEOWNER'S POLICY

The insurance policy is a contract between the policyholder and the insurance company. A homeowner's policy is issued to individuals who intend on living in the home they are insuring.

These policies are multiple line policies that provide coverage to the building structure, personal property, and additional living expenses. I will go into more detail on these coverages in future chapters.

When a claim is filed, at least one or more of these coverages may be affected. On a large fire for example, all three coverages usually apply. It is important to understand them and how payment is issued on each of them from your insurance company.

To make it simple to understand, in the policy under building structure coverage, your policy typically covers so many types of losses that it lists only the items that are *not* covered if you have a loss. Under the personal property coverage, it is exactly the opposite. It lists specific losses that are *only* covered. If any loss outside of this list occurs, there is no coverage.

The additional living expense coverage is designed to help relocate you during the period of time that your home is being reconstructed. It can pay costs you incur above and beyond the normal costs you would pay. For example, if your electric bill is normally $150 a month and now between the house getting repaired and your temporary house your electric bill is $250, the insurance company will pay the difference of $100.

There is so much more to these coverages than the quick overview I just explained. As I mentioned, I will discuss them in more detail later in my book. I just want you to be aware of them now, for I will be referring to them throughout the book.

The contract between the insurance company and a policyholder has duties listed that both parties must abide by. I will be reviewing just a few of the key ones that a policyholder needs to be aware of once a claim is filed.

a. You need to contact the insurance company promptly once you are aware that a loss has occurred. Once a loss has occurred, decide if it is worth filing a claim as discussed earlier, and if so, call your insurance company immediately. I recommend calling your insurance agent. It is best to alert him or her that you are filing a claim. If the office is closed, the recording will either forward your call to the company's twenty-four-hour claim center or give you a toll-free number to call.

b. You need to protect your property from further damage. If your roof has a hole in it, put a tarp on it and keep the receipt. If your window was broken, have it boarded up. You want to show the insurance company that you tried your best to stop the damages from getting worse.

c. Take photos and make notes of all damaged items. Document what you are claiming damaged including your personal property. If half the contents in the living room are damaged, remove and protect the undamaged portion and photo and document the damaged items remaining. The burden is on the policyholder to establish value on these personal belongings. That is why keeping purchase receipts and warrantee books on appliances can be very helpful in establishing value.

There are many other duties that are important in your policy. I believe these three are the most important to perform *prior* to the claim representative arriving at your home. If any of these are not done properly, you could negatively affect the outcome of your claim and open the door for the claim representative to question the extent of damages throughout your home. Don't get off on the wrong foot!

THE INSURANCE AGENT

The insurance agent is probably the number 1 tool for generating revenue for an insurance company. Although commercials and catchy slogans can hook a future policyholder, it is the insurance agent that reels them in. To give you an idea of how many agents are out there, one major insurance company states that if you add together the first and second largest fast-food chain stores you see on the streets today, they have more insurance agent offices than both franchises combined. That's a lot of offices! That's a lot of personal contact with policyholders! That's a lot of potential revenue!

The insurance agent is not only well respected within the insurance industry but also regarded by the policyholder as the insurance company. If a claim goes well, the policyholder believes the agent did a great job looking out for him or her. If there are conflicts, delays, and issues between the policyholder and the insurance company during the claim process, the insurance agent is expected to get involved and make things right. Or else!

The reality is that most insurance agents have very little say so in the claim process once it begins. At best, they can call the adjuster and ask for updates. For all practical purposes, the claim representative does not care how many policies the policyholder has or how much premium dollars he or she pays each year. The claim representative is not supposed to let that influence his or her decision making when handling a claim.

The insurance agent does not always share this philosophy. They are *very* aware of the multiple policies a policyholder has and tend to be more active on claims where a long-time profitable policyholder is involved. Is this fair to newer policyholders who have only one policy and file a claim? Remember, insurance agents are running a business. They truly want the best for all individuals, but like any business, they need to make sure the policyholders with larger accounts are very happy too. Interesting, isn't it? Food for thought . . .

You will rarely hear a policyholder say a bad thing about their insurance agent—until a claim they filed is denied. Then all bets are off. Once the claim representative explains the denial to the policyholder, their first response quite often is, "My insurance agent sold me this policy and never told me this was not covered!" I cannot tell you how many times I have heard that over the years.

The reality is that many insurance agents are not fully aware of all the coverages, exclusions, and endorsements within the policy. That is the role of the claim representative—to explain these areas to the insured *at* the time of the loss. This does not help a policyholder a great deal *prior* to filing a claim or even at the time he or she signs a contract with the insurance agent.

Even if the agent knew the policy inside and out, it would be almost impossible to explain all the things that can go wrong to a home and what is and is not covered when the policyholder signs a contract with them. Remember, the insurance agent's main focus is to sign new business. Not to explain the policy cover to cover. Right or wrong, good or bad, this is a reality that becomes very apparent once a claim is denied. Policyholders have left insurance companies shortly after being denied on a claim due to this lack of information. Unfortunately, a policyholder will probably not get any more information up front from a different insurance agent if he or she switches to another insurance company.

Most insurance agents give you a copy of your policy at the same time or shortly after you sign a contract. It is not easy reading by any means. Just the fact that you receive it should not mean you are accountable for understanding your own policy. It takes a claim representative a long time to grasp the coverages and information inside the policy.

Make sure you keep the policy available in case you have a loss. Consulting with your agent prior to filing a claim can prove to be helpful. If he or she does not know the answers to your questions, they can find them out relatively quickly. Also, hiring a company or individual that is very knowledgeable on the homeowner's policy once a claim has been filed can help you throughout the claim.

THE CLAIM REPRESENTATIVE

I want to state once again before I start this chapter that I am not defending or attacking the claim representative's position or any specific individual. I have the greatest respect for claim representatives and know their job is not an easy one. They can be a hero on the first claim of the day by writing a check for damages and be a villain on the last appointment because they had to deny the claim. This group of individuals has to work face-to-face with policyholders and perform inspections in some of the worst environmental conditions that one can be in (fires, floods, sewer backups, etc.). That being said let us continue on . . .

It is very interesting how people can take a particular seminar or class, be presented with the same material, and leave with completely different views on what was taught that day. They internalize the information, apply it to their own experiences, and decide how they will apply that information in their lives.

Claim representatives go through extensive training during the first year of their career. Policy language, estimating damages to buildings, and customer service training are just a few examples of topics they are taught. With all this standardized training, it is still highly likely that if you assigned the same claim to two different claim representatives, they would not only handle the claim differently but may also come up with a different conclusion.

I found that no matter how standard or objective training is or how black and white an insurance policy is, a claim representative's subjectivity still plays a role in the handling of claims. I heard frequently over the years, "No two claims are alike. Handle each claim on its merits." This means that a claim representative needs to take in and process the damages he or she sees and then interpret how the policy applies in the given situation.

Although this is the best approach for a claim representative, it opens all kinds of doors for interpretation and is usually the starting point of conflicts within the claim process.

A typical claims department within an insurance company is well diversified with a wide range of different personalities. The goal of the supervisor over that department is to ensure consistency in its claim handling and to make sure estimates are written accurately and policies are interpreted correctly. You can imagine how challenging this can be when each claim representative has their own approach to handling losses and perception of damages and how they relate to the policy.

For example, a claim representative early in his or her career handles a large fire loss with extensive damages to the policyholder's personal property. Once the proper forms are filled out to document the loss, the claim representative must evaluate it and compare the list to items he or she saw during the initial inspection. At this point, he or she notices that there are very expensive large items listed that were not seen in the home. The representative goes back and re-inspects and realizes after discussing these items with the policyholder that they were never there.

Being a claim representative and handling a loss like this, especially early in his or her career, can leave an individual with a very negative view on what *can* happen on large personal property losses. Unfortunately, for many claim representatives, it can leave a lasting impression that has him or her going into similar losses very cautious and overly suspicious. This frame of mind can damage the relationship between the claim representative and policyholder from the start. They may demand receipts on all items. They may insist on physical evidence that the item was there even in a fire that completely destroys the home.

These types of negative experiences early on can affect a claim representative's decision making on building structures, personal property, and even the additional living expense coverage.

For example, a claim representative allows a policyholder to stay in a hotel until a temporary home can be found. Several homes are presented to the policyholder as an option, but none are satisfactory. Weeks go by and the family is still in the hotel. They tell the claim representative they like it there and enjoy the pool and room service and really do not want to leave. The claim representative realizes this was the cause for the delay, not that the homes were unsatisfactory. The family finally chooses a temporary home and moves in to it.

On the next claim he or she handles, a family needs to be put into a hotel. The claim representative tells them they have five days to stay there and must have a temporary home chosen by the end of that period of time. The family is shown two or three homes that are either too far from their children's school or from where they work, so they do not choose any of these homes. Due to the experience the claim representative had prior, he or she tells them they better move quickly because their time is running out. This pressure forces the family to pick a temporary home that is in a bad neighborhood or far from work. They are unhappy throughout the claim process due to the pressure to leave their hotel after five days.

These are real stories that have happened during the claim process. A claim representative makes decisions daily based not only on the training they have but also on the past experiences they have gone through. This subjectivity is almost unavoidable and plays a role in every single claim that is handled. It can aid a person to make the correct decision or cloud one's judgment and make a poor one.

The claim representative, unlike the insurance agent, has the most control over the outcome of the loss during the claim process. It is very important for a policyholder to ask questions and expect decisions to be made on a timely basis. A policyholder should ask for deadlines on when estimates will be complete and how long it will take to process the damaged personal property list. When that time has passed, phone calls should be made to the claim representative asking for the status. If every time you call, you are told to call him or her back in another week, your claim is probably not being worked on as it should.

I believe expectations are everything. If you go to a five-star restaurant and the service is less than perfect, let them know. Not only verbally but also through the tip you leave. If you are getting your oil changed and the shop is supposed to vacuum your car and they don't, let them know. People should be held responsible for their word. Especially when they advertise service above and beyond.

Most insurance companies advertise that they will be there for you when you need them most. They will give you exceptional service and treat you fairly. Hold them to it. If you do not get a response from a claim representative within the given time frame they laid out for you and you can't reach them or keep getting delayed, ask for a supervisor. Remember, the squeaky wheel gets heard. No claim representative wants complaints on their files. Many may keep delaying the payment due to busy schedules and the need to work overtime to keep up. This is not and should not be your problem.

I want to end this chapter by stating that most of the claims that are handled by claim representatives are handled very quickly, smoothly, and fairly. The quantity of satisfied policyholders after going through the claim process greatly outnumbers the claims with complaints. It seems like all we hear about are the complaints. It can definitely misrepresent the hard work and commitment that a claim representative has toward his or her function within the insurance industry.

As a policyholder, be prompt with whatever documentation is requested. Make yourself available for the claim representative to meet at the house and discuss the claim. Do everything that is asked of you in a timely fashion. This way, you have not delayed the claim process, and the burden is given back to the claim representative to process your claim quickly and arrive at a proper resolution.

THE CONTRACTOR

Choosing a contractor to reconstruct your home after a loss is the first major decision you will make during the claim process. The claim representative will ask you during his or her initial conversation if you have chosen one. Most policyholders have not put much thought into who will do the repairs. They are so busy trying to handle the hectic world around them that repairs are not a priority at this time.

There are several reasons why a claim representative is asking if you chose a contractor. First, they want you to know that it's time now to think about who will complete the repairs to your home. Second, for the insurance companies who recommend contractors, this is their chance to explain their contractor program to you and explain the advantages for using them.

What are some of the *advantages* that will be explained to you by your claim representative for using a recommended contractor?

a. The claim representative does not want complaints on quality of work or timeliness of repairs throughout the claim process. Many recommend a contractor to avoid such issues. This may not be explained to you, but it *can* motivate a claim representative to recommend a contractor.

b. Typically, the policyholder does not have to worry about directly paying the contractor. All materials are reimbursed directly to the contractor throughout the reconstruction. Once the work is completed, the policyholder must sign a statement stating that they are satisfied with the work performed, or the contractor will not get paid for the labor he is owed. This can be very motivating to a contractor to complete the work in a timely fashion so they can be paid.

c. Most contractors receive quite a bit of work through this referral program. If they perform poorly on a loss, this could jeopardize future referrals. Hence, affecting their revenue considerably.

d.   Once a policyholder chooses a contractor that a claim representative refers, if there are issues that develop during the reconstruction, the claim representative can usually contact directly the person in charge and get the issue resolved.

e.   This is a referral from the insurance company. Most contractors you will meet shortly after your loss have not been referred to you. The claim representative is inferring, "I know this company. They have done work for policyholders in the past. They are capable of doing the reconstruction on your home."

What are some of the *disadvantages* when using a contractor that is referred by an insurance company?

a.   The contractors that are referred to the most on these programs receive a very high volume of claims each week. Most of these contractors, even if their workload is too great, will rarely say no to new assignments. If they do, they may get passed by on the next possible loss because they turned down prior work. This plays a major role in how quickly your repairs are completed. Many of these contractors take longer to reconstruct your home than contractors not on the referral program. This impacts when you can move back to your home especially in cases where you have been relocated due to a large fire.

It also plays a role around significant dates and events in your life. You may be told prior to repairs that the work will be complete, and you will move back to your home before Christmas. Or before the new school year begins. By them not reaching their projected dates, it can disrupt your lives even more than this tragic event already has.

b.   The payment system to contractors on the referral program for the labor they are owed can be quite restricting to the contractor. Although they may receive an advance, they are supposed to finance the labor for the entire reconstruction job with their own money until the job is complete. On larger losses, it can slow the work down due to little funds available to continue. Remember, your loss is not the only one they are working on. They are financing the labor on many other projects at the same time.

c.   When a referred contractor is assigned, they know they will get paid when the job is done. There is less motivation to alter from the original repair estimate and do upgrades or additional work in your home. These changes can be a nightmare for a preferred contractor because they need to justify the new materials and additional labor they are spending to the insurance company / claim representative. There are many instances where they cannot justify them, and they do not get paid for them. In those cases, they lose money on the job.

Using your own contractor with the money issued from the insurance company gives you much more flexibility in choosing how and where the money is spent. For example, the insurance company does not mind if you shift money from the damaged living room over to the damaged kitchen. They both were affected by the fire. But if you choose to put carpet in a basement that was not damaged by the fire, the insurance company will not pay for that.

d. One issue that a claim representative tends to point out when discussing the use of a referred contractor versus the policyholder's own contractor is that they guarantee the labor for five years on the referred contractor. They also stand behind them, making sure the work is completed.

Most contractors will guarantee their work for five years if you discuss it with them. They will put it in writing in their contract.

You have to realize that these referred contractors are not employed by the insurance company. They are completely independent from the insurance carrier. If there were any serious issues between you and the referred contractor and you were to file a complaint against the insurance company, they may ultimately not be responsible. It would be between you and your contractor. Hence, there may be no difference between you hiring your own contractor or a referred one when it comes down to dealing with major legal issues you may encounter.

e. This is probably the most compelling argument in the industry for not using the contractors on the referral program. And also one that is very hard to document its validity. A claim representative may not refer a contractor because they are the quickest and most qualified. They may refer them because over the years, a "professional relationship" has developed between the two of them. The claim representative may be forwarding business to "help increase the growth" of the contractor.

This "relationship" is *not* encouraged by the insurance company. The referral of these contractors is supposed to be objective and unbiased. One indication that the claim representative is referring "his or her" construction company is if the contractor arrives with the claim representative when he or she first meets with you. This action is *not* sanctioned with the insurance company. No contractor should be pushed or given a sales pitch from a claim representative. If this occurs, you should alert a department supervisor of this activity.

If the claim representative, during his or her first conversation over the phone with you, tries to influence you in using a particular contractor, this is inappropriate as well. These two scenarios should immediately alert you of a possibly *inappropriate* relationship between the claim representative and contractor, and you should consider using your own.

Within the first twenty-four hours of a policyholder's loss, their emotions are running wild. They are not only homeless but have also lost most or all of their personal belongings. I refer to this state of mind as a deer in a headlight syndrome. Most are so overwhelmed that they just stand there staring in a frozenlike state, unable to thoroughly comprehend what is happening around them.

This is the perfect time for many contractors to approach a homeowner and pursue them to sign a contract. After a large fire occurs, either the same day or early the next morning, there will be numerous public adjusting firms or contractors sitting in their cars waiting to approach the homeowner. The stress this puts on a homeowner is incredible.

I am amazed how many homeowners sign a contract after talking to the first PA firm (public adjusting firm) or contractor they meet. Why do they sign immediately? They are in this *syndrome* state of mind and are easily persuaded. What should they do?

Several months ago, I went looking for a new car. After a day or two, I decided on what make and model I wanted. But every car dealership I went to had only one or two of those cars on the lot. I remember thinking, "I wish one of these dealers would have seven or eight of these cars so I could compare mileage, exterior and interior condition, and custom upgrades and have a better color selection."

Having all these contractors and public adjusting firms right outside your home is your chance to see what they all have to offer. Compare them to each other, and make a sound decision. Although intimidating and quite overwhelming, it is a great opportunity.

Most of these individuals are capable of negotiating your claim with the insurance company and reconstructing your home. But they are here for one purpose: to have you sign a contract. How do you sort out the good from the bad and ugly?

Keep in mind the following points:

1. Listen to them carefully. If they spend more time discrediting the insurance industry than explaining what they can and will do for you, *"red flag"* them. I would not consider using them. They are more interested in playing on your emotions than helping you get your life back together.
2. Ask if the person you are talking to is a sales representative or the owner of the company. A sales representative, once the contract is signed, is on to

the next fire. You will probably never see him or her again. An owner will probably not meet with you again either, but he or she can give you more insight into the company. Also, if you get his or her business card, you now have a direct line if you choose his company to call for future issues. No one likes complaints. An owner can make the proper calls during reconstruction and get the crew back on path.

3. Most larger contractors or PAs like to bring in managers from all their departments when they meet with you. These individuals oversee specific operations within the company. This can be a bit intimidating at times, but it is good to see that they have a management team that run their crews. These managers will probably be the people you deal with throughout your loss.

What questions do you ask them?

1. How long have they been in business? A company that has been in business for only two years can be just as qualified as one that has ten years' experience. Just make a note of the years. It all plays a part at the end of your decision-making process.
2. Have they done reconstruction on large fires before? How many? How often? Make sure you are not dealing with a handyman who wants *you* to be his first large fire! Ask how small and large the fires were that they worked on. How long did it take to complete the work? If a contractor tells you they do three or four large fires a month, I would tend to avoid them. They are probably very busy, and your reconstruction will take twice as long to complete.
3. Ask if you can see homes that have recently been completed. You can ask for references, but you will never get a name and phone number of someone who was unhappy. You can call them if it brings you peace of mind. Although you will never see a completed home that looks poorly done, you can at least see their quality of work and picture what you may like to be done in your home.

These contractors and PAs want you to sign a contract with them immediately. This way, they have a commitment from you in writing, and you will then dismiss the other contractors due to having chosen your own. Do not rush into signing contracts.

As these contractors meet with you one by one, ask these basic questions I have outlined. Keep these points in mind as well. Weed out the ones you dislike, or "*red flag*" them and move on to your top choices. Then schedule appointments the next day every two to three hours at a specific location *you* designate. Do not let them take control of the meeting by bringing you to their office or a restaurant. Talk more in detail with them and find out what they will do for you. Will they do upgrades to your home? Will they remodel your basement the way *you* want it done? If they agree, tell them that if you sign a contract with them, you want these upgrades in writing along with the contract.

Meet with them all, and then later that week, make up your mind. I promise you that the pressure to sign a contract immediately will be intense! They may promise the world for you, but keep them honest. Tell them, for example, that you will not sign a contract unless you get these upgrades in writing.

Manage and control the outcome of *who* you select to do the reconstruction. Your house is one of the biggest investments in your life. Once they start working on your home, they will be *your* contractor for the next four to six months. You want it to go as smoothly as possible.

Before I continue, I need to explain the role a mortgage company plays during the reconstruction process. Most homeowners have a mortgage on their home. These mortgage companies have an insurable interest in the home and want to make sure all repairs are completed. Their name, along with yours, is typically put on all building repair checks over $10,000. The amount may differ based on the mortgage company's guidelines.

If a policyholder chooses to use his or her own contractor, the check issued from the insurance company needs to be signed by you and forwarded to the mortgage company. They then usually issue one-third back to you to apply toward the initial repairs/demolition of your home. After you have completed one-third of the work, they send an inspector out to review the repairs. Once they confirm that the work is completed, they issue another one-third. This amount is used to complete the rest of the repairs. Once the job is finished, they will send an inspector out again, confirm the work is done, and release the final one-third.

Although these one-third payments can be at times a challenge for some construction companies, they know going into the project, they will receive money throughout the job, and it will help ensure that work will continue with little financial strain. This is an advantage over the referral program because it keeps money flowing throughout the project versus waiting until the end to get reimbursed for the labor.

MANAGING YOUR BUILDING LOSS CLAIM

The previous chapters introduced you to all the key players you will be dealing with throughout your claim process. The insurance company, the insurance agent, the claim representative, and the general contractor. I wanted you to understand the impact they each have during the claim process so you can better understand the following chapters.

Let us assume that at this point you have filed a claim, a claim representative has scheduled an appointment to meet with you. What's next?

Let us first establish what kind of loss you have suffered. Since a large fire affects most or all coverages in a policy, we will use a large fire as the cause of loss. One of the first things the claim representative will do when arriving at your home is to take photos of all the damaged areas. Included in the photos will be both the structure and personal property damages. His or her main goal initially is to gather information.

Most of the larger insurance companies have several types of claim representatives. The two main groups are the *line unit* claim representatives and the *large loss* claim representatives. The line unit rep tends to handle smaller to medium-size losses. This does not mean that they are incapable of handling a larger loss. These large losses are very time consuming and better handled by a large loss team who handle losses of greater size. There is no official dollar amount that is documented in your policy that determines when a large loss team may be used. Typically, when the structure damage exceeds $100,000, the team is called in to handle the loss.

Usually when a claim is filed and a large fire has been noted, the line unit rep is first to examine the scene. They take photos and note significant information that will aid the large loss team prior to arriving at the home.

This process of first meeting the line unit rep and then the large loss team can be a little confusing to the policyholder. The homeowner walks through the loss with the line unit rep and explains what happened, where they were at the time of the fire, where they believe the fire started, and what structural and content damage they noted, and then they repeat this process again for the large loss team. Many policyholders ask, "Why is a line unit rep coming out when you already know it is a large loss? Just send out the large loss team." I think it is a valid point. Many of the large loss teams want to make sure it truly is a large loss and want to get a feel of how long they will be out there. So the line unit rep sends them information prior to their arrival.

The line unit rep should explain the claim process to you after they examine the home inside and out. They should explain what the large loss team is going to do—who makes up the team and the fact that they will be making decisions hereon out for the duration of the claim process.

If a large loss team is not going to be called in, the line unit rep may begin his or her detail assessment of damages immediately. This first contact with the line unit rep is very important. It is *your* first impression of your insurance company, and hopefully, it will be a good one.

An advance can and should be issued, if it has not already, toward replacing personal property that you need immediately. Clothing, food, and hotel stay are just a few items that the claim representative should be giving you money for. Although your insurance agent tends to let the claim department handle all advances, they have authority to issue you a check for emergency purposes. Do not hesitate to ask them for it at the time you file the claim if you are now homeless and do not have clothes to wear for your family.

The main difference between a line unit rep and a large loss team is that the line unit rep will handle most of the claim on their own. He or she will explain building coverages, damages, personal property replacement, and your temporary housing.

A large loss team will have several adjusters at your home, measuring rooms, taking photos, and drawing diagrams of the interior of your home. They will also have a content specialist whose only job is to help you process your damaged personal property.

Once the large loss team arrives and they complete their scope or assessment of damages to your home, the claim representative in this team who has been assigned to your loss will ask you several questions regarding the loss. He or she may ask you prior to scoping the home. Scoping simply means writing down all the damages to your home. These questions may seem very direct or infer that you may somehow be responsible for the fire, but they are not meant to be. The claim representative will be asking standard questions that are needed to further investigate the loss. Be honest with them. Even if you fell asleep smoking and that started the fire, accidents like this are covered in your policy.

The two main reasons why a loss may not be covered are (1) the policyholder intentionally started the fire and (2) the policy was not enforced on the date the loss occurred. For the most part, there should be coverage. Remember, fires that are started through acts of stupidity are still covered. Example, you accidentally place hot charcoal in a garbage can next to your garage, and the garage burns down shortly after. This is a covered loss.

When a large fire occurs, the insurance company will usually hire a cause-and-origin firm to investigate where and how the fire started. If they find that an appliance or product was responsible for the fire, it may be possible to pursue the manufacturer for reimbursement toward damages to your home. This is called subrogation. The insurance company pays for this service. The cause-and-origin investigators will also ask you many questions pertaining to the loss. Once again, be honest. If you do not know the answer, tell them. Do not guess.

The insurance company normally would like to be the first to walk the fire scene and note all damages. They may tell you that they do not want anyone walking through the home and disturbing the evidence. If they tell you this, do what they say. You do not want to jeopardize any part of the claim because you did not follow their instructions.

But in most cases, if you have hired a contractor, they do not have a problem with them writing an estimate prior to the insurance company's arrival. I would recommend this. If your contractor meets the claim representative with a detailed estimate of what needs to be repaired, it can work to your advantage. In my opinion, it can greatly affect the final outcome of the settlement.

Claim representatives have very busy schedules. Anything that can make their job a little easier can go a long way. Especially if the estimate you present to them is written on the same computer program as the one they use. Your contractor has then done most of the work, and all the claim representative needs to do is make notes and create his or her own estimate using the contractor's estimate as a guide.

Computer programs allow a claim representative and contractor to create a detailed estimate noting almost every possible repair that can be completed in an average residential home. Some of these programs have some limitations when it comes to writing small losses, large commercial losses, and homes with many custom designs. But for the most part, they are a very good tool to negotiate building damages with insurance companies.

So now the claim representative has documented everything needed to process the building estimate. You have talked to the content specialist and cause-and-origin investigator. Your contractor has written an estimate and has discussed it with the claim representative. What's next?

As I stated previously, I will cover personal property damages and additional housing expense in the next two chapters. We will focus on the building structure presently.

Before the claim representative leaves your home, ask him or her when the estimate will be completed. Make a note of it. When that time arrives, follow up with a phone call. Depending on his or her schedule, most claim representatives should be able to have it completed within two weeks of inspection. This time span may vary depending on the claim representative's workload and the time of the year the loss occurs. Many vacations are scheduled during Christmas and New Year. It could take up to thirty days before you receive an estimate if a loss occurs during this time.

Once you receive the estimate from your claim representative, forward it to your contractor for review. He may notice that some of the items he included in his estimate were excluded in the claim representative's estimate. The contractor needs to prepare a rebuttal and resubmit. This should be done as soon as the contractor receives the estimate. The sooner a rebuttal is handed in, the greater the chance the claim representative will review it right away since he just sent his or her estimate out to you.

Your contractor and claim representative have now come to an agreement. In rare cases where an agreed settlement cannot be made, an appraisal can be done to help bridge the gap between both estimates. A third party will walk with both estimates through the home and arrive at a recommended settlement. Good communication and accurately writing the damages in the home by both the claim representative and the contractor should avoid the use of an appraisal.

Once all parties agree on the settlement, the claim representative will, if he or she has not already requested it, ask for a tax and demolition form to be filled out. This form checks to see if any back taxes are owed on the building. It also verifies if the city will request money to be held back prior to issuing the policyholder a check in case the owner decides to abandon the property. Usually, there are not back taxes or amounts held back from the city. But it can and does happen.

The claim representative will also ask you to fill out a proof of loss form prior to issuing any payment. This form is simply a statement that states that both you and the insurance company agree on the settlement amount on the building estimate. It is wise to include with this form a short letter stating that as the reconstruction proceeds, more damages may be found and the final settlement amount may increase. This just helps document the fact that at this point, you agree with the insurance company, but there may need to be a revision in the future. The proof of loss needs to be notarized before sending it back to your insurance company.

Once these two forms are received by the insurance company and their investigation has concluded, they will issue a check. The policyholder and mortgage company will appear on the check. The insurance company has no obligation to put the contractor's name on the check even if they have a contract between you and the contractor. The policy is clear that the only names that should be on the check are those who have an insurable interest in the property. But most insurance companies with a signed contract will add the contractor's name on the check.

Whoever is listed on the check will need to endorse it and forward it to the mortgage company. As explained in an earlier chapter, the mortgage company will send out one-third of the total check and inspect the home prior to issuing any more funds.

Depreciation is an important topic to understand. This topic was briefly explained as well in a prior chapter. The claim representative should be asking the policyholder while writing his or her scope how old the various building materials are throughout the home—from the drywall, carpet, floor tile, wallpaper, windows, cabinets, electricity, light fixtures, etc.—so an accurate percentage can be taken for depreciation.

Very few claim representatives ask these questions on *all* those building categories. By not inquiring about it, it is impossible to ensure that all categories are being depreciated accurately. Most claim representatives have a set amount in their head before writing the estimate of how much they will depreciate.

To ensure proper depreciation has been taken, a policyholder needs to review the estimate after it is written and note that on newly installed categories like windows, for example, no depreciation is taken. If you go through and identify over depreciated items and point them out to the adjuster *before* the initial check is issued, they should revise their estimate. This will increase the amount of money you will receive up front and decrease the final replacement cost held until the job is complete.

The final replacement cost is simply the amount of depreciation that has been deducted from your estimate. Most homeowner's policy allows you to receive this amount once the job is complete.

Code upgrades are usually an issue during the reconstruction of a home. Once the city inspects your home shortly after a fire, they note various areas in your home that violate current code requirements. Code upgrade allowances are additional money above and beyond the limit established in your policy, usually a predetermined percent that can be applied to these specific violations. Most homeowner policies have some form of code upgrade in them. In many instances, 10 percent of the total insured value can be applied.

Once all code-related repairs have been done, your contractor needs to submit a detailed estimate to your claim representative explaining how and where the money was distributed. After review from the claim representative and all issues and questions are addressed, a check can be issued for these repairs. Many claim representatives tend to wait until the job is complete before issuing the code upgrade check. Discuss this with them. They can issue it once an agreed settlement amount is established.

Lastly, when the work is completed or near completion, a final addendum needs to be submitted by the contractor to the claim representative for all damages found *after* the original agreed-upon estimate was established. The claim representative will usually walk through the home for one last inspection, ensuring that all work paid for was completed. The final addendum will be added to the total settlement, and the final replacement cost check will be issued.

The main point I want you to learn from this chapter regarding estimates and contractors is to submit to the insurance company an estimate that is accurate and based on the damages resulting from the fire. This estimate should not be a wish list of all the upgrades you want throughout your home. Those upgrades need to be negotiated with your contractor once the final settlement amount is determined. That is why I encourage using your own contractor. They tend to be more flexible with upgrades and revisions.

There is a big difference between an estimate that is written very detailed, thoroughly noting all damages and repairs that need to be made, versus an estimate filled with inaccurate and overstated damage and repair costs. They may both arrive at the same final dollar amount, but the latter of the two will only cause tension with the claim representative and delay the issuance of the final settlement.

MANAGING YOUR PERSONAL
PROPERTY LOSS CLAIM

A large fire in a home can quickly destroy your personal belongings. You have so much money and memories invested in these items located throughout your home.

This topic is one of the most important ones covered in my book. Why? Briefly, (1) you cannot hire a general contractor to process your contents like you can for building damages and tell them to write an estimate and submit it *without* your involvement, (2) your personal time has to be invested in the processing of these damaged items to ensure all are accounted for, and (3) the mortgage companies have no insurable interest in your personal property. Their name will not appear on the check—only the policyholder. When you receive the check, it's yours to spend.

Most major insurance companies have at least one specially trained claim representative that processes the data that you submit and inputs it into a personal property inventory form. Many have, as discussed in the prior chapter, a large loss unit that has a content specialist that will inventory for you, at no additional charge, your personal property loss.

Many policyholders choose to allow the content specialist to inventory their damaged items. Many hire a company to process the contents for them. These companies charge you a percentage that is applied to the total when the list is complete. They can charge up to 3 percent. Although you are paying for this service, these companies are very determined to write every penny down that you lost so the final figure is as *high* as possible.

One advantage for hiring a company to process your loss is that you can feel confident that when they are inventorying your contents, they are working on your behalf to get you maximum settlement. They not only enter all the information into an inventory form but also look up prices to ensure current values are being submitted.

Although the content specialist does almost the same thing, their lists may not be as thorough as the hired company's. When you have a company who gets paid based on the final totals of a content list versus a person inventorying for free and getting paid on a weekly salary, there is an obviously different mind-set going into the inventory process. That does not mean the content specialist does a poor job. But they may not be quite as thorough.

Please note that no matter whom you use, you need to get involved and walk each room affected by the fire. Do not glimpse at the completed inventory list and see a lot of items recorded and say, "Looks like they have everything." I have seen this happen on so many claims.

The best way to manage and control the outcome of your personal property loss is to be there, all day if necessary, and work side by side with whoever you use to help you. If a room is completely burned up and nothing but piles of rubble lay on the floor representing your personal belongings, no one but *you* can decipher what is there. Do not attempt to inventory your contents by yourself if you have a large fire. It is very overwhelming, and it will take you months versus days with a professional company.

When it comes to submitting your damaged personal property list to the insurance company, quicker is always better as long as it is done carefully and thoroughly. The average time insurance companies take to determine settlements on personal property losses after it is submitted to them is at least one month. The content specialist typically only handles a portion of the claim. It usually goes from them to a specialist who then verifies the prices of the items you submitted. Prices on expensive electronics, appliances, furniture, and collectibles are all researched by the insurance companies.

Make it clear to the content specialist that you may have overlooked some items and forgotten to put them on your list. Open the door to the possibility that if you do think of more items, you will be submitting them to the insurance company to add to their already-received list. This *will* happen to you, and you need them to expect more items in the near future.

If the insurance company can find the same item you wrote on your inventory list for less than what you put in as the current value, they can either order it for you or cash you out for the lesser value. Many policyholders do not mind the items getting ordered. It saves them time having to go to the store and buying it themselves.

In the chapter on sample forms, you will see a sample of a personal property inventory form. These forms are very generic and can be submitted to most insurance companies. It is very important to fill out the first six columns for each item. Briefly list them by room—the quantity, description, model number, store you purchased it from, age, and price of each item.

Sounds like a lot of work? It is! And if any information is missing, it not only can delay the processing of that particular item but also possibly delay the entire inventory form from being processed depending on how much information is missing.

All six of these columns are important. Make sure you have the correct quantity for each item, and price them out with current values. The one column that impacts the overall initial payment of the inventory form is the age of the item. I know it does not seem to be that important, but it is critical that this is filled in and accurate.

Depreciation, once again, plays a big role in determining what you will initially get paid. Be honest with the ages or years that you purchased the items. Just keep in mind that the older the items are, the less you will get paid up front for their replacement. This was discussed in a previous chapter.

Most content specialists, if asked how they determine how much depreciation to apply on each item, will say that it is based on its age and what type of item it is. For example, a two-year-old television set will be worth more at two years than two-year-old baby clothing. The expected useful life span for both is different. So do not expect all two-year-old items to be depreciated the same throughout the inventory list.

The problem policyholders have with insurance companies is when the content specialist is computing depreciation on contents; they *cannot* show the policyholders the depreciation guide that is used to calculate the amount of depreciation. This guide is meant to be for internal use only and not meant for the public to see. It lists thousands of items and gives the average life span for each and every one of them. Although most content specialists may verbally refer to this guide to justify their depreciated amounts, try asking to see it. It will never be shown to you.

Many content specialists will go to a loss and see that the clothing is older and depreciate a specific percent on the whole category. For example, 60 percent depreciation may be applied across the board because the clothing is several years old, and it is easier to process them with the same percentage throughout the inventory form.

This is not the correct way to depreciate. If the deprecation guide was made public to all policyholders, you would see a major change throughout the entire insurance industry regarding how personal property is depreciated. Policyholders would never permit this abuse to happen.

Once you receive the completed personal property inventory form from the insurance company, you will see several totals at the bottom of the page. The three most important ones are (1) how much money you are getting now, (2) how much money the entire inventory form came to, and (3) how much is being held aside until you replace the item.

No matter how it is justified from the insurance company, if for example, your total personal property inventory form is $75,000 and the amount you receive after depreciation is $20,000, it is very unlikely that you are going to be able to collect the total owed to you. There is just too big of a gap between both numbers. If you question it, the response will probably be, "It's based on the ages of your items. I have no control over the final outcome."

Keep copies of all inventory forms submitted and look over all items carefully once you receive the completed form. Review newly acquired items and ones purchased less than a year ago. See how much depreciation was applied on those items. Look for groups of items with different ages being given the same depreciated percent (50 percent across the board). Your contents should not be depreciated in this way.

Once you start replacing items that are on the inventory form, you need to save the receipts and keep track of the specific items you replaced. For example, you purchased a television that you had in your bedroom. The TV is listed on line 10 under Susan's bedroom. Take the receipt and write line 10 on it. Then note on *your* copy of the inventory form that you replaced that item, and circle the amount owed to you.

If you have listed on your inventory form that a new lamp will cost $200 and you were given $150 after depreciation, you are now owed $50. But you have to actually spend the $200 in order to collect that money. The receipt you submit has to be at least that amount, or you will not collect the entire amount owed. For example, if you only spent $175 for the lamp, you will only get $25 more because you only spent $25 more than the original $150 you received.

The *concept* of being able to receive the depreciation back on an item is a great benefit. Let us say you have a ten-year-old car and the blue book is only $5,000 currently. A new car identical to yours is $15,000. Imagine walking into a dealership and getting full price for your ten-year-old car. Sounds crazy! Receiving the depreciation back on an old item is a great benefit offered on most policies.

The problem with this system is that it takes a lot of discipline to keep receipts, track all purchases, and send in batches of receipts periodically to the insurance company. Especially when you receive so little money after depreciation on so many items throughout your inventory form.

Once again, make sure newer items are not depreciated, and be organized with the receipts and paperwork while replacing items to maximize the amount of depreciation you can collect.

Besides replacing damaged personal property, the insurance company allows and pays for the cleaning of salvageable items that were covered with smoke but not destroyed. These items include your clothing, furniture, and art—basically everything that was not damaged or burned.

This can be a great benefit especially if due to replacing damaged items, you are getting close to your limit of coverage.

Both your building structure and your personal property have limits that each are insured for. If your contents are insured for $100,000, then you have up to that amount to claim all damaged (replaced) items and cleanable items. If your damaged totals are at $89,000, for example, and you have the option to clean many additional items in your home for $10,000, it is wise to do so. Then all your contents will be addressed, and you will be within your policy limits.

One of the goals the content specialist will have when they meet you for the first time is to discuss the packing up and cleaning of your contents. Just like the building structure, they may recommend companies to use and state, "If you use someone else, we cannot do anything about the items that don't come clean." They may add, "If you use our referral, these companies only pull items that can come clean."

This once again is incorrect. Even companies that are referred by insurance companies have items that are rejected. If there is any chance of being able to clean the item, they will pack it up and take it with them. These rejected items are later added to the personal property inventory form and reimbursed to the policyholder. The insurance companies will do the same thing with the companies you use when rejects are submitted.

Do what makes sense when it comes to the cleaning of your contents. If you have no recommendations for cleaning companies, go ahead and use their referrals. If you like a particular cleaning company or the firm you hired refers a company, use their recommendation. Most of the cleaning companies will clean your items properly. What does not come clean can usually be added to your damaged personal property inventory list, and you will be reimbursed for it.

MANAGING YOUR ADDITIONAL LIVING EXPENSES

Unlike the building structure and personal property coverages that have limits assigned to them, the additional living expense coverage or ALE typically has no limit. ALE will cover any necessary increase in living expenses throughout the reconstruction period. This includes hotel stay, your relocation and temporary housing, additional food, and utility bills. Although there is a form insurance companies use to calculate these expenses, many claim adjusters try and simplify the process. This makes it easier for everyone involved.

There are two main questions you need answered immediately after a fire occurs and you are now homeless: (1) Where am I going to live? (2) How am I going to pay for my housing, food, clothing, etc.?

Most policyholders stay with friends or family the first couple nights. Or they check into a hotel. Credit cards are a useful tool to use for spending. It is not only convenient but you can also submit later documentation that you did actually spend this money during the first twenty-four to forty-eight hours. These are the two quickest solutions given the situation you are in.

As explained earlier, call your insurance agent immediately. If their office is closed, you will be either connected to a twenty-four-hour claim center or given their toll-free number. These claim representatives are well trained and can give you good advice and guidance.

It is important for you to understand that the insurance company will pay for any *increase* in your living expenses. For example, if you normally spend $150 a week between groceries and going out to dinner and during the hotel stay you are spending $250 a week, you will be paid an additional $100. Many policyholders do not understand this concept.

The thought process is you already spend $150 a week. Now the additional food expense is $100. The insurance company understands that you are inconvenienced during the hotel stay, but they can only pay the increased amount over what you normally would spend. Many policyholders submit all their receipts during the hotel stay and question why all are not reimbursed. This is why. Only the increase above and beyond your normal expense will be paid.

This is very important because early in the claim process, the claim representative will ask you how much you normally spend each week on food and groceries. Some policyholders inflate the amount. This ultimately goes against you because now you will have to spend more before you get paid for the increase on your food expense.

As I have said throughout my book, be honest with the information you give the insurance company. They will compensate you for all increases in your living expense.

Another point is being organized. Keep a folder or binder for all documentation you are given and for what you save during the claim process (receipts, for example). The only reason many policyholders do not get reimbursed for increased expenses is because they forget to save receipts. Maybe three or four family members are working and going to school, and all are buying food, emergency clothing, etc. Receipts are frequently lost or never saved. The insurance company *cannot* make you whole if you do not submit everything to them. Remember that.

Many insurance companies will tell you that gas for your car is not reimbursed. This is incorrect. If your hotel or temporary home is located *farther* from your children's school or work than your home is, you can get reimbursed for the additional mileage. Once again, you need to document how many miles you normally drive a day and show them the increased mileage you are now incurring.

Once a policyholder arrives at a hotel shortly after the fire, you should tell the hotel manager that you are a fire victim and needs shelter until you are relocated. Many hotels offer a discount to fire victims. They will ask for your credit card, and you will need to hold the room just like you would in checking in to any hotel.

Soon after you check in, make every effort to contact your claim representative, and tell them where you are staying. If you know you do not have enough funds on your credit card to pay for the hotel stay, the claim representative can contact the hotel and have them fax or e-mail the final bill directly to the insurance company. They should make arrangements to settle the bill before you check out.

If a claim representative has not been assigned yet, call the twenty-four-hour claim center and ask which local office is handling your claim. Then call the local office and ask who has been assigned the loss. Most claim representatives are on appointments. They may not know they just received a new loss. By calling the local office, the claim representative will be contacted and told they were just assigned a fire and the homeowner is trying to get a hold of them.

You have been paying insurance premiums for years. This is the time when your insurance company needs to be there for you. Do not hesitate to call your insurance agent or the local claim's office. The squeaky wheel gets heard! It's time to squeak!

Once you are contacted by the claim representative, one of the first subjects you need to discuss is an *advance* toward buying clothing and food. Especially if one was not given to you by your insurance agent. Advances can and should be issued. Many claim representatives prefer to see the loss first and get an understanding of approximately how badly your home and personal property were damaged. It is important that you give them an accurate estimate when you first talk with them. For example, you may say, "We lost half of our personal belongings." Or, "All of our personal belongings on the second floor were burned by the fire." This gives the claim representative a clearer picture of the severity of the fire.

An advance is exactly what it says. It is money given to you up front and will be deducted from your final personal property inventory form once that amount is determined. Why deducted? Why not just given to you? The purpose of the advance is for you to purchase items you lost in the fire. Because they were damaged, you will be submitting them on your personal property inventory form. If the advance is *not* deducted from the total, you will be reimbursed twice for the items.

This is important to understand because all these lost items you are purchasing *now* need to be added to your damaged content list *later*. You need to save receipts and submit them at the same time that you submit your completed content inventory. This way, when the advance gets deducted from your totals, you will not get shortchanged by the adjustment.

Now you are in a hotel, and you have been given an advance, and the claim representative will make arrangements to pay for your hotel bill. What's next? A temporary home or apartment needs to be located. Does the policyholder have to find a place? No. Can they? Yes.

You will be confronted with two choices to make: (1) stay with family and friends during the reconstruction period or (2) stay in an apartment or home. Which one should you choose? This is a very important decision to make and possibly the most important one that directly affects you and your family during the claim process.

When a large fire first occurs, the homeowner usually receives a lot of support from family and friends. Family members may offer to house you throughout the reconstruction. This period of time is very stressful for you, and by having the support of loved ones around you, it can ease the pain.

The insurance company can and will compensate you for living with family members. The compensation is really for increased utilities and inconveniences incurred to the household and policyholder. There is no hard written formula to establish the amount issued. They will not ask for documentation of current utility bills from your family and pay differences each month. They usually determine a per-day cost and multiply it times thirty days and issue a monthly check. For example, they may offer $25 a day for thirty days—$750 a month.

You may think this is low because normally, rent for a four-bedroom furnished home is double. The reality is you are not paying rent. You are living there, spending the same amount of money monthly for food, and the household is incurring minor increases in utility.

The biggest disadvantage to living with relatives is over time, after five or six months, tension arises. Everyone stops being polite and starts getting in each other's way. Privacy is also a problem. On almost every loss I handled where the policyholder's family moved in with relatives, I received calls within thirty to sixty days stating, "We have to move out or we will kill each other!"

I do not recommend staying with relatives over a long period of time. It may work out during the initial phase where a hotel would normally be used but not in the long run. The additional living expense coverage offers temporary housing. Use it.

Another option a policyholder has is to find an apartment or home that someone is renting. Especially in the current economy, many homes that were once listed to sell are now being rented. If you find a home that is conveniently located, present a lease agreement to the insurance company. As long as the home is similar in size and number of rooms as the home you own, they will pay the rent.

Some of the disadvantages of finding your own temporary home are the amount of time you have to spend locating these homes and finding ones close to your current residence. Also, they usually do not come furnished. You would have to find a company to furnish it and submit more contracts to the insurance company.

The most popular method of housing is to use a company that not only locates homes and apartments but furnishes it as well. These housing companies also get paid directly from the insurance companies. You do not have to worry about paying rent each month.

Most insurance companies have worked with housing companies over the years. They know what their general rates are each month and have gained trust in them and their services.

A policyholder will probably be presented with business cards of housing companies soon after the loss occurs. Although these companies may deliver good service, I would leave all my options open. References are very important when choosing a housing company. Remember, this is your family, wife, husband, and children that you are entrusting someone to take care of.

Neighbors, family, and friends are usually *not* a good source for getting referrals on a good housing company. The best referrals are through your insurance company and through the company that may be representing you.

An independent firm that you hire to represent you will know housing companies. They have probably sent many fire victims to these companies. There is probably a referral rebate sent from the housing company to the firm you are using to show their appreciation for referring them. This is common practice between many housing companies and representing firms.

Whenever money is transacted between two parties, the question that always arises is if the firms are using the housing companies because they are top in the industry or because they acknowledge the referral with a referral rebate. Food for thought . . .

Using a housing company the insurance company recommends usually works out very well for the policyholder. Although the insurance company may have an agreement to get lower invoicing from these companies, the service level is very high. The fact that the costs are lower for the insurance companies does *not* reflect on the service the housing company provides. Once again, these housing companies are not employed by the insurance companies. They are independent of them.

These housing companies will call your hotel and have them bill their company direct for the overnight stays. That means you will not have any charges on your credit card, and the claim representative does not have to issue any checks to the policyholder. It is easier for everyone. The temporary homes are usually found quickly, and most homeowners find one they prefer within twenty-four to forty-eight hours from the time the search begins.

Furnishings are delivered to the home and picked up once the family moves out. The family is able to function the same as if they were at their own home. These homes will also have the same number of bedrooms and bathrooms as before. This can quickly help the family regroup and start focusing on the rest of the claim process.

It is important to point out that the policyholder, in this temporary home, is now a *tenant*. Just as any rental home or apartment, there is a security deposit owed to the landlord. This deposit is usually *advanced* from the insurance company so the policyholder does not have to pay out of pocket this expense.

Here is that word *advanced* again. What does this mean? The insurance company will pay the security deposit but will deduct it from the total settlement on your personal property inventory form once determined. Why? Because you are now a tenant and responsible for respecting not only the rental unit you are now living in but also the furnishings as well. Once your home is repaired and you move back, the landlord will walk through the home and access the property. If it is in the same condition as when you moved in, they will forward you your security deposit back. If there are, for example, carpet stains or holes in the wall, a repair fee will be determined and taken off the security deposit. You will then receive only a portion of your deposit back.

The same process is done for your furnishings. The company that supplied the furniture, televisions, washer and dryer, etc., will examine the items and determine if there are any damages to them.

The golden rule for a family living in a temporary home or apartment is, "Treat the home and furnishings *better* than you would treat your own." You want the whole security deposit back at the end of your stay. Keep that in mind!

HOMEOWNER'S CLAIM BINDER

The purpose of this section is to instruct you on how to create your own organized, personalized claim binder. This tool will be kept near you throughout the claim process and will contain all the pertinent information you have collected during this period of time. Having a personalized system set up to keep track of all documents is very important.

A fire victim may stay overnight at a relative's home, later move into a hotel, and finally settle into temporary housing, getting phone calls at any time of the day and any place. Typically, an individual will scribble information down on a scrap of paper and place it in his or her pocket hoping to find it at a later date. Unfortunately, these scraps are often lost, and important contacts you have made are gone with them.

This claim binder is the best solution to avoid losing documentation throughout your insurance loss. Let us begin.

The following materials are needed prior to setting up your claim binder. All can be purchased at any office supply store:

- A two-inch, three-ring binder (any color)
- 8 ½ inches × 11 inches in size
- A binder pocket on the inside of both the front and rear covers to hold pens and misc
- Tab sheets to separate various topics
- Plastic sheets with pockets to hold photos of fire damage, structure, and contents—similar to a photo album
- Plastic sheets with pockets to hold business cards
- Lined sheets of paper with three holes for insertion into the binder ring
- Three-hole punch for new materials received that need placement in the binder

Once you have all the necessary materials, it is time to create your claim binder. Organize the tabs in the following order:

1. *Claim information*: This category needs to be *first* in your claim binder. It contains important, specific information about your policy—your claim number, policy number, policy limits on structure and personal contents, and your deductible. All this information will be given to you by your claim representative. Include the name and contact number of your insurance agent and claim representative in this section. This page will be referred to quite frequently, especially during the first week of your loss.

2. *Contacts*: Except for your claim information section, contact names and business cards of significant individuals throughout the claim process is probably the most referred-to category in your claim binder. Organize the business cards by *type of business*, placing them inside the plastic business card-holder sheets. For example, on one page, you may have all contractors; the next, all housing companies and cleaning companies. This way, you can focus on one group of individuals at a time that have common interests. You will find this extremely helpful when needing to find a number or person quickly. You may even want to make brief notes on a business card, rating them on who you prefer the most . . . the least.

3. *Correspondence*: Here is where you place all outgoing and incoming letters to and from individuals during the claim process. Keep them sorted as well. Keep insurance letters separate from temporary housing updates. Keep them organized by date with the most recent on top. You may want to use minitabs to separate the insurance company letters from other company letters inside this main tab. Whatever works for you.

4. *Emergency item list*: Soon after a large fire occurs and a homeowner has lost most or all of their personal belongings, they start thinking of the prescriptions, cosmetics, baby formula, dog food, etc., that were lost and need immediate replacing. At the end of this chapter, you will find a list of the most common emergency items that will be needed prior to temporarily moving in with relatives or a hotel. Keep this list at the beginning of the tab to help remind you of your immediate needs. *Do not* try and wipe off the soot on these items to salvage them. They will most likely be contaminated and need to be disposed of with the rest of your damage contents.

5. *Photos*: This tab section is designed to feature the photos that capture the "worst of the worst" of your structure and content damages. You will probably take hundreds of pictures and may want to get a separate photo album for the majority of them. Feature all the elevations of the exterior of your home first. Then work your way into the home, following an organized path through your house and taking photos along the way. Organize these photos within this tab in the same order as you entered the rooms from the entrance of your home.

This technique of organizing your photos helps to clarify later where it was taken when referred to in the near or distant future.

6. *Building estimates*: Here is where you insert both your insurance company's structural estimate as well as your own contractor's bid. You may get several revised and renegotiated estimates as well. Keep them organized with the most recent dated ones on top. Only estimates regarding *structural damage* are in this tab. I would advise a clear plastic page with a pocket to put all receipts of building materials purchased by you to secure your property in this section.

7. *Personal property lists/inventories*: This is one of the most important tabs regarding future reimbursements from the insurance company within your binder. It will contain the following: (a) a list of damaged contents you and/or an outside firm created to submit to the insurance company; (b) the personal property inventory form the insurance company forwarded to you outlining the payments you received and detailing how much you are eligible to receive in the future; and (c) as you collect receipts and send them to your insurance company to receive the replacement cost on specific items, you should be going into this section of the binder to note on *your* copy of the personal property inventory form which item you sent the receipt in and how much you are requesting reimbursement for. You also need to have several clear pages with pockets to file all receipts on items you have purchased. At the end of this chapter, there will be several rooms listed that are standard in an average home, listing personal property within each that are typically placed in them. This will be of great value when confronted with a room so severely burned that you cannot recognize all items still remaining.

8. *Additional living expense*: There will be several items in this section: (a) any receipts saved for additional living expenses during the temporary housing duration (food/gas, etc.); (b) hotel bills and credit card statements; (c) a rental lease between the landlord and yourself and a rental lease for the furniture you are using within your rental unit; and (d) the contract between the housing facility and yourself permitting them to make all the arrangements for you. Once again, keep several clear pages with pockets for all food and gas receipts.

The previous eight categories represent the most widely used tabs a homeowner may create within the claim binder. Feel free to add categories or expand within a tab. This is *your* personalized claim binder. The more comfortable you feel using it, the more you will refer to it and the better organized you will be.

The following are lists of emergency items that may need to be replaced immediately:

EMERGENCY ITEM LIST

HEALTH
medications/drugs
medical supplies or devices
glasses or contact lenses

PERSONAL CARE/TOILETRIES
Cosmetics
shampoo/conditioner
soap/body wash
razors/shaving gel
curling iron
combs/brushes
deodorant
lotion
toothbrush/toothpaste

CLOTHING
shirts/pants
blouse/slacks
shoes
socks/undergarments

ELECTRONICS
cell phone/charger
laptop

MONETARY ITEMS
Cash
Checkbook

FOR INFANTS
formula
bottles
diapers

FOR PETS
food
water bowls
medications
lease
waste disposal bags

HOUSEHOLD ITEMS
facial tissue
trash bags
household cleaners
soap
laundry detergent
blanket/pillows
bottled water

PERSONAL ITEMS
credit / debit cards
identification IDs
driver's license
wallet/purse

BUSINESS ITEMS
briefcase
client contacts

PERSONAL PROPERTY

The claims process involves preparing an inventory of your damaged personal property and determining the cost to repair or replace each item. The following are some tips on how to complete your personal property inventory form.

- Group your items by room, starting left to right, from the floor upward toward the ceiling. If the items in a particular area are completely burned, close your eyes and visualize what was there, and write it down based on your memory.
- Remember to inventory items that may be stored in out-of-the-way locations, such as the attic, crawl space, garage loft, and tops of closets.
- When inventorying electronics and appliances, make note of model numbers, MFG numbers, serial numbers, brand names, and store locations where they were purchased. The item may be so burned you cannot identify these numbers. By noting the store, it may be a brand name they carry, and researching the price will be easier. Note minor details as well. For example, DVD and VHS player with built-in self-recording capability.
- Group certain items together. For example, ten pairs of socks, twenty pairs of T-shirts, six towel sets, etc. These can be written on one line. When inventorying makeup or over-the-counter medicine, put down one set price. For example, makeup, $150; cleaning product, $75; spices, $50. Avoid one-line entries of greater dollar values. For example, adult/men's shoes, $1,500. Since each pair may range differently in value, group these items by price. For example, gym shoes, $65 each; dress shoes, $85 each.
- If you choose to price these items yourself, you can research the replacement costs by utilizing the following:
  1. Websites of retailers or manufacturers.
  2. Newspaper ads—never sale prices, only regular retail prices; when you go to purchase these items later, they may not be on sale at that time.
  3. Original appraisals especially on jewelry/watches.
  4. Gift receipts/personal receipts.

5. Walking through department stores and writing prices off the shelf, noting model numbers/brand names.

6. If you have a special item like a collectible figurine and you are having trouble finding the price, quite often with details of the item, the insurance company's replacement service will be able to locate the price.

7. If you go to one electronic or furniture store to locate all the identical or similar damaged items, salespeople will walk with you and help you create this list. It is very helpful for you and a possible large sale for the salesperson if you choose to purchase the items there. Don't be afraid to ask for help.

PERSONAL PROPERTY HOUSEHOLD ITEM LIST

The following lists are items that are typically kept in these known locations. Obviously, there can be additional items that are not listed here that may be in your rooms. Keep in mind that contents can be defined as any item you will take with you when moving out of your home. If the item is installed in your home, it will be a part of the structure. If the item is usually installed, for example cabinets, but were taken out and are now sitting on the floor in your basement, they would be considered contents.

ATTIC/BASEMENT/STORAGE AREAS

- Window air-conditioner
- Books
- Old cabinets or new ones not installed yet
- Dehumidifiers
- Space heaters
- Portable fans
- Freezer
- Refrigerator—wine and regular
- Furniture
- Pool table
- Slot machine, game tables
- Holiday decorations
- Keepsakes
- Ladders
- Luggage
- Tools / workbenches
- Sports equipment
- Toys
- Storage trunks
- Vacuum cleaners

BATHROOM

- Bath mats
- Bath accessories
- Bed linens
- Curling iron
- Candles
- Clothes hampers
- Cosmetics
- Cleaning products
- Curtains
- CDs
- Draperies
- Electric toothbrush
- Electric appliances
- Hair dryers
- Incense
- Medicine
- Organizers
- Potpourri
- Portable mirror
- Paper products
- Pictures
- Rugs
- Radio or CD player
- Soap dish
- Scale
- Shower rod
- Tables
- Toiletries
- Towels
- Telephone
- Wall art

BEDROOMS

- Window air-conditioner
- Bed frame
- Bed—foot and headboard
- Bed—mattress / box spring
- Bedding
- Blankets
- Comforters
- Compact discs
- Blinds/shades
- Bookcases
- Books
- Bureaus
- Computer
- Chairs
- Chests
- Clocks
- Curtains/draperies
- Decorative items
- Desks
- Dressers
- DVD player
- File cabinet
- Jewelry
- Lamps
- Mirrors
- Planters
- Nightstand
- Dressing table
- Printer
- Pictures/paintings
- Pillows
- Rugs
- Radio
- Sheets
- Stereo equipment
- TVs
- Tables
- Toys (children's room)

FAMILY ROOM/LIVING ROOM

- Blinds/shades
- Bookcases
- Books
- Briefcase
- Cabinets
- Chairs
- Chests
- Clocks
- Computer
- Couches/sofas/love seat
- Curtains/drapes
- Cushions
- Coffee Table
- Desks
- Entertainment center
- Fireplace fixtures
- End tables
- Footstool
- Lamps
- Laptop
- Mirrors
- Musical instruments
- Piano
- Pictures/paintings
- Planter
- Printer
- DVDs, CDs, videos
- Rugs
- Recliner
- Stereo equipment
- Surround sound system
- Tables
- Television sets
- Vases
- Wall units

DINING ROOM

- Blinds/shades
- Buffets
- Rugs
- China cabinets
- Chairs
- Chests
- China
- Crystal
- Collectibles
- Candle set—centerpiece
- Curtain rods
- Cloth napkins
- Curio cabinet
- Glassware
- Lamps
- Linens
- Mirrors
- Pictures
- Paintings
- Planters
- Portable bar
- Place mats
- Serving pieces
- Sideboards
- Silverware
- Tea or coffee sets
- Serving table /cart
- Silk arrangements
- Tables
- Tablecloths
- TV tables
- Liquor

EXERCISE ROOM

- Barbells
- Books
- CDs and DVDs
- Clocks
- Dumbbells
- Drinks
- Exercise equipment (other)
- Nautilus machine
- Pictures
- Posters
- Plants
- Rowing machine
- Scale
- Stationary bicycle
- Stereo equipment
- Small refrigerator
- Television
- Treadmill
- Mats
- Magazines
- Mirrors
- Towels
- Exercise videos
- Watercooler
- Weight plates
- Yoga mats

HOME OFFICE/STUDY

- Answer machine
- Appliances
- Business supplies
- Books
- Bookcases
- Briefcase
- CDs and DVDs
- Camera
- Computer
- Computer accessories
- Collectibles: stamps/coins
- Chairs
- Desks
- Fax machine
- Fireplace equipment
- Files
- Filing cabinets
- Lamps
- Laptop
- PDAs
- Paintings
- Photographs
- Manuscripts
- Plants
- Printer
- Radio
- Rugs
- Scanner
- Stock, bonds, securities
- Stereo equipment
- Tape recorder
- Tables
- Telephones
- Television

LAUNDRY ROOM

- Brooms
- Cleaning supplies
- Laundry detergent
- Dryer
- Dustpans
- Duster
- Door hangers
- Dish towels
- Floor mat
- Fabric softener
- Floor shampooer
- Hangers
- Hampers
- Iron
- Ironing board
- Ladders
- Laundry bags
- Mops
- Pet food
- Paper products
- Portable vacuum
- Rugs
- Stools
- Scrub brushes
- Table—folding clothes
- Vacuum cleaner
- Vacuum attachments
- Wire racks/shelving—portable
- Washer
- Wet vac.

PORCH OR PATIO

- Bug spray
- Bug zapper
- Brooms
- Chairs
- Cushions
- Candles
- Decorations
- Fly swatter
- Fire extinguisher
- Fans
- Lamps
- Lawn chairs
- Tables
- Umbrellas
- Rugs/mats
- Loungers
- Lawn games
- Outdoor cooking equipment
- Outdoor cooking utensils
- Outdoor sporting goods
- Statues
- Stereo equipment
- Speakers
- Planters
- Pool supplies
- Pool toys
- Patio lights
- Jacuzzi tub
- Jacuzzi chemicals

GARAGE / SHED

- Automobile products—oils, antifreeze, windshield solvent
- Bicycles
- Brooms
- Carpentry tools/supplies
- Furniture
- Fertilizer
- Garden tools/supplies
- Gasoline
- Hedge trimmer
- Luggage/trunks
- Ladders/step stools
- Lawn chemicals
- Lawn mower
- Leaf blower
- Lawn spreader
- Miscellaneous flooring supplies
- Outdoor games
- Paint and supplies
- Portable racks/shelving
- Pool toys/chemicals
- Rakes
- Sports equipment
- Small boats
- Sprinklers
- Scooters
- Toys
- Trailers
- Wheelbarrow
- Workbench
- Weedwacker
- Tools
- Tarps

MEN'S CLOTHING/MISC

- Belts
- Briefcase
- Boots
- Coats
- Formal wear
- Gloves
- Golf clothing
- Gym bag
- Hats and caps
- Jackets
- Jeans
- Neckties
- Nightwear
- Raincoats
- Pants
- Scarves
- Shirts
- Shoes—gym and dress
- Slacks
- Sports jacket
- Swimsuits
- Suits
- Tennis clothing
- Ties
- Socks
- Sweaters
- Sweatshirts and pants
- Underwear

WOMEN'S CLOTHING/MISC

- Belts
- Briefcase
- Boots
- Blouses
- Coats
- Dresses
- Furs
- Formal wear
- Gloves
- Golf clothing
- Gym bag
- Hats and caps
- Handbags
- Hosiery
- Jackets
- Jeans
- Lingerie
- Neckties
- Nightwear
- Raincoats
- Pants
- Scarves
- Sandals
- Shirts
- Skirts
- Shoes—gym and dress
- Slacks
- Sports jacket
- Swimsuits
- Suits
- Tennis clothing
- Ties
- Socks
- Sweaters
- Sweatshirts and pants
- Underwear

CHILDREN'S CLOTHING/MISC

- Belts
- Boots
- Coats
- Gloves
- Gym bag
- Hats and caps
- Hosiery
- Jackets
- Jeans
- Neckties
- Nightwear
- Raincoats
- Pants
- Scarves
- Snow clothes
- Shirts
- Shoes—gym and dress
- Slacks
- Sports jacket—children
- Swimsuits
- Suits
- Tennis clothing
- Ties
- Socks
- Sweaters
- Sweatshirts and pants
- Underwear

PERSONAL PROPERTY INVENTORY FORM

Although every column on the personal property inventory form or PPIF is important, the first six columns are the ones you are responsible to fill out *prior* to submitting it to the insurance company. A copy of a standard PPIF is shown at the end of this book so you can follow along with it while reading the following information.

The following are instructions on how to fill out the first six columns:

1. *Rooms*: There are several ways to list the rooms in your home that contain the damaged contents. It is best to either start upstairs and work down or the opposite way. Write them down in the same order they are situated in the house. For example, if the master bedroom is the first room at the top of the stairs and the bathroom is next to it, write down master bedroom and then bathroom. Remember, the claim representative will be walking through your list. They need to be able to follow it easily.

   You may label the rooms as either bedroom 1, 2, 3 or Mom and Dad's room, Michael's room, Sarah's room, etc. Labeling the rooms with family names can be helpful for you later when reviewing the inventory forms.

2. *Quantity*: When filling out the quantities, list the "each" price of the individual items. The program the insurance company uses will automatically extend the totals out. The only time you should put one in the column is when you have one item, or you are submitting one price for a group of identical items. For example, one line for cosmetics, $100.

3. *Description of property*: Write down specifically what the item is. Try to be short but detailed. For example, 32-inch flat-screen TV with built-in DVD player. Many times you have an unusual item such as a large wicker planter with silk flowers in it. If you purchased the items together, write it down that way. If separate, list them as two entries on your inventory form. Quite often, you may have no idea what to call an item. It was a very unique gift or an item

purchased on vacation. Do your best and remember that someone else has to be able to read this line and understand what it is you are claiming damaged.

4. *Manufacturer/brand name*: This is a very important column that needs to be filled out correctly. It mostly applies to appliances and electronics. But if there is a model number on any other item, list it. The retail industry is frequently discontinuing electronics after a few years. They come out with updated versions with more gadgets on them. The item you purchased two years ago may not be carried any more in retail stores. By writing down the model number and brand name, the insurance company will be able to find the new model that replaced the old one. Even if it is a little more money and has more gadgets on it, you are entitled to receive it.

Most insurance companies have purchasing agreements with large retail stores. They may research pricing, for example, at one large electronic store. By doing so, if you choose to order the items through them, the retail store discounts the price. This saves thousands of dollars for the insurance company, and you still get the item you listed on your inventory form.

Quite often, you will not be able to read the model number or brand name from the electronic item. It will be so badly damaged that no identification will be made. In this case, describe the item as detailed as you can, and try to write down an accurate price. The insurance company can determine a price by comparing your description with other similar items and get you an item very close to what you had.

Documenting model numbers and brand names are one area insurance companies stress on. Many homeowners do not fill this out properly, and the claim representative has to come back out and reinventory all these items. It will delay the processing of your personal property inventory form and may increase the frustration level of the claim representative. Try to be thorough and avoid delays and conflicts.

5. *Date of purchase or age:* Although this may not seem very important to you, it is critical to the insurance company and has the greatest impact on the overall inventory form. Here is where depreciation plays a role in your damaged contents. As previously explained, the older an item is, the less value it currently has.

Some homeowners, realizing this fact, tend to write down that most of the items are new or one year old when in fact, they are much older. As I have stated many times, be honest with the age, and give an accurate year or date of purchase. Listing older items as new or just purchased on many lines will delay the processing and increase tension between the claim representative and yourself. Once the trust between both of you is broken at any point throughout the claim process, delays and frustrations will increase.

Write down either the month or year or how many years ago the item was purchased. For example, February 10' or the age, one year old. Either one is acceptable with the insurance company. Remember, every single line entry has to have an age or date of purchase. If the line is DVDs, for example, and you purchased the items over many years, write down a range: one to four years old. They *should* depreciate an *average* price for them.

As discussed in a previous chapter, once you receive the completed PPIF from the insurance company, review it carefully. Check the age of the items, and make sure that on clothing, for example, the claim representative did not use the same percent of depreciation on the whole category. It should be based on the age and estimated useful life of each line item, not on the whole category alone. If you have a full-length leather coat that is two years old and baby clothes the same age, they should not be depreciated the same. Baby clothing has a much shorter life span than *dressy* adult clothing.

If you believe that items have been *over depreciated*, make notes on a copy of your PPIF and resubmit it for review to your claim representative. An adjustment should be made. Ask for a copy of the form *prior* to them issuing a check. Once the claim representative has issued a check, it is unlikely they will revise their depreciation and issue another one.

Remember, only your name will be on the insurance check. The mortgage company has no insurable interest in *your* personal property. You want as much money *up front* as possible to aid you in the replacement process.

6. *Replacement cost*: This is a very important category because any depreciation applied will be deducted from this price. If your price is low, you will not only be *shortchanging* yourself but the money you receive after depreciation is applied will be lower as well.

It is important to understand that the insurance company owes you for the *current* price to replace the damaged item. Not what you paid, for example, five years ago. This can be a real challenge because many homeowners have no idea what these items are selling for now. Some items were purchased on vacation or were gifts where no receipt was given.

Many homeowners close their eyes and try to remember what they paid for the item. Bad idea! Researching the prices on the Internet or walking through a store that sells similar items are the two best ways to get pricing—both of which take a lot of time to do. This is one of the best reasons to use a firm that will price these items for you. They have staff members that do nothing but establish value on a wide range of items.

Never use sales prices when noting the value of damaged contents. They probably will not be on sale at the time you need to replace them. The insurance company understands this and expects you to use regular retail prices.

If you are listing DVDs or CDs and the price varies on many of the items, either separate them on two different lines by price or take an average value for the item. DVDs and CDs are usually depreciated 50 percent the moment the item is taken out of the case.

The remaining columns are designated for the insurance company to fill out. Briefly, here is a summary of those columns:

1. *Depreciation Percent*: This is where the insurance company establishes a *percent* to depreciate an individual line. This *percent* should vary throughout the inventory form based on the age and type of the item. Review this column carefully to ensure accurate depreciation.
2. *Tax percent*: Prior to submitting your completed PPIF, you need to inform the insurance company on what the tax rate is in your city or township. This amount will be applied to all items listed. Write it down at the top of the form in the space provided above the tax percent column. If the tax is different for food or medicine, make a note on the individual line in the tax percent column.
3. *Replacement Cost (R/C)*: This column is the extended total of each of the items you submitted. Either at the top or bottom of that column, you will see the grand total. This is how much money your total personal property loss came to.
4. *Depreciation $:* This column is the amount of depreciation applied in terms of *dollars* versus a *percent* as in the previous column. It specifically states the amount of money being withheld for each line item. It will also have a grand total, allowing you to see how much money was depreciated on all your submitted damaged contents.
5. *Total this settlement:* This column lists the differences between the replacement cost and the depreciation on each item. The grand total of this column should be the amount your insurance check will be. The check may be less if your deductible is applied to the total. It may also be less if you have a specific limit

on a category. For example, jewelry and furs usually have a limit established for them per your policy. It may be $1,500 per item and $2,500 for total items. So if you have one piece of jewelry valued at $2,000, the limit of $1,500 would apply, and you would only get $1,500 instead of the $2,000 you listed for that item. Discuss special limits with you claim representative. Most homeowner policies have special limits on specific categories of items.

6. *Replacement cost benefits remaining:* This column should be the same total as the depreciation column. It is the amount of money being held back on each item, and this column also has a grand total. You receive this money once you submit a receipt showing you paid the total replacement cost on each item.

That is why it is very important to put the line number down from the PPIF on each receipt and circle the replacement cost benefits remaining that you are requesting reimbursement on. It will make it easier for your claim representative to identify the amount and issue payment to you. It is best to collect several receipts and send them in *batches* instead of one item at a time. This way, you are receiving larger checks and can apply this money toward the replacement of other items on the inventory form.

The final two pages that accompany the personal property inventory form are (1) the total summary page and (2) the summary page.

The *total summary page* details out the totals of all the columns and special limits applied in the PPIF. It is a great reference tool for a quick overview on what has been paid out and what is being withheld. Please note that the term *actual cash value* is simply the replacement cost minus the depreciation. It should be the same amount as the total this settlement column.

Claim representatives will often state that the amount of money you receive initially is the ACV amount paid out on a content inventory loss. Please note that if the ACV amount is higher than the limit established in your policy for personal contents, the total settlement will be less than the ACV total. The limit indicated in your policy will then be issued.

The *summary page* will detail out each room that was recorded on your PPIF and the total amount of damages for each room. It also details out special limits applied with totals of all the significant columns on this form.

Once again, you have three choices on who can fill out a personal property inventory form: (1) the insurance company's content specialist, (2) an adjusting firm, or (3) yourself. No matter who does it, you will need to be involved in order to ensure all items are accounted for. Hiring an adjusting firm will save you quite a bit of time and allow you to focus on other issues that you will be confronted with throughout the claim process.

PERSONAL PROPERTY INVENTORY

Date of Loss:

Claim Representative:

Claim Number:

Insured:

Coverage B Limits:

Total Personal Property Inventory — $0.00 ... $0.00 ... $0.00 ... $0.00 ... $0.00

Rm#	Qty	Description of Personal Property	Mfr/Brand Name	Date of Purchase or Age	Replacement Cost (Each)	Dep %	Tax %	R/C	Depreciation	Total this Settlement	R/C Benefits Remaining
						0%		$0.00	$0.00	$0.00	$0.00
						0%		$0.00	$0.00	$0.00	$0.00
						0%		$0.00	$0.00	$0.00	$0.00
						0%		$0.00	$0.00	$0.00	$0.00
						0%		$0.00	$0.00	$0.00	$0.00
						0%		$0.00	$0.00	$0.00	$0.00
						0%		$0.00	$0.00	$0.00	$0.00
						0%		$0.00	$0.00	$0.00	$0.00
						0%		$0.00	$0.00	$0.00	$0.00
						0%		$0.00	$0.00	$0.00	$0.00
						0%		$0.00	$0.00	$0.00	$0.00
						0%		$0.00	$0.00	$0.00	$0.00

	PERSONAL PROPERTY INVENTORY FORM				
	DATE:				
	Repair or Replacement Cost	Depreciation	Actual Cash Value	Settlement	Maximum R/C Benefits
TOTALS	$0.00	$0.00	$0.00	$0.00	$0.00
		EXCESS OF SPECIAL LIMITS		$0.00	
		EXCESS OF COVERAGE B LIMIT		$0.00	
		DEDUCTIBLE		$0.00	
		NET CLAIM		$0.00	

Summary Page

Room Totals			
Bedroom 1	$0.00	Attic	$0.00
Bedroom 2	$0.00	Carport	$0.00
Bedroom 3	$0.00	Exterior	$0.00
Bedroom 4	$0.00	Game Room	$0.00
Den	$0.00	Garage	$0.00
Dining Room	$0.00	Hall Bath 2	$0.00
Entry/Foyer	$0.00	Laundry Room	$0.00
Family Room	$0.00	Loft	$0.00
Hall	$0.00	Miscellaneous	$0.00
Hall Bath 1	$0.00	Office	$0.00
Hall Closet 1	$0.00	Other	$0.00
Hall Closet 2	$0.00	Patio	$0.00
Kitchen	$0.00	Porch	$0.00
Linen Closet	$0.00	Shop	$0.00
Living Room	$0.00	Storage Room	$0.00
Master Bath	$0.00	Utility Room	$0.00
Master BR	$0.00		

Special Limits		Amount of Loss	Limit
Home Computer (HC)		$0.00	$0.00
Business Property (BP)		$0.00	$0.00
Money (MO)		$0.00	$0.00
Trading Cards (TC)		$0.00	$0.00

Total Replacement Cost:

Total Replacement Cost Benefits:

Total Replacement Cost Benefits Paid:

CONCLUSION

The purpose of this book is to help you understand the overall claim process. With this increased understanding, you will better manage and control the overall outcome of your insurance claim. Policyholders should be better prepared *prior* to experiencing a devastating loss and know what is entailed when filing a claim with their insurance carrier.

Once again, this book is not meant to attack or defend the insurance industry or target a specific group. There are enough books in circulation that do this already. After reading this book, one should not feel like they were being steered one direction or the other—to or from the insurance industry or, more specifically, their own insurance career.

The claim representatives and insurance agents play a critical role within the insurance industry. The insurance agent's sole job is to generate new business. The claim representative solely generates an expense for the company. Both positions appear to be on opposite sides of the spectrum when looking at the financial books. But both have the same goal to deliver outstanding customer service to the policyholders. I find that very interesting.

They are the only real personal contact an insurance company has with the policyholder. Training is forever ongoing for both individuals as well as adapting to policy changes and new ideas that are constantly being implemented that affects their day-to-day decisions and schedules.

The pressures to either increase sales and/or control expense are also driven deep into their minds every day. There are internal payroll cuts that can put additional pressure on them and make it difficult to not only deliver outstanding customer service but also to keep up with the daily paperwork that never seems to slow down.

Is it right that these internal pressures within an insurance company can affect the level of service a policyholder may receive? Is it right that a bad experience a claim representative may have with a policy holder can remain in his or her memory and result in a subjective or even slightly prejudiced decision on a similar loss? Is it right that contractors will still accept new losses through the referral program even when they cannot handle their current load just to ensure their future referrals will not be in jeopardy?

No. It is not right. It is reality though and something that each policyholder needs to be aware of once they have a loss and begin the claim process.

One last word of inspiration. Having your home and personal property damaged due to any significant loss is a tragic event. No matter how prepared or educated you are prior to a large loss, you will still experience so many intense emotions and high levels of stress. The period of restoration, although maybe four to six months, will feel like it lasts forever.

Keep reminding yourself that your home will be completely remodeled at the end of the reconstruction. Even with a soft real estate market, your home will be worth top value because so much will have been replaced and updated. Living in your home will be like starting over. No untidy rooms or spoiled food or outdated product in your refrigerator or kitchen cabinets. You now have a newly remodeled basement to spend time with your friends and family members.

Also, most of your personal property will be new. A new flat-screen television will now hang on the wall in your family room. A new living room set and kitchen appliances will await you. You will now have either replaced or dry cleaned clothing to hang and organize the way you have always wanted in your closets.

After months and years go by, it will be a memory that you will look back on and tell friends, "I would not wish a large fire on my worst enemy!"

I hope you can also say, "I am glad I read this book. It really helped me manage and better control the outcome of my insurance claim!" Good luck and God bless!